Digital Elixir: Harnessing the Power of Artificial Intelligence

Mazen Kaldas

Published by Mazen Kaldas, 2023.

DIGITAL ELIXIR: HARNESSING THE POWER OF ARTIFICIAL INTELLIGENCE

First edition. July 12, 2023.

ISBN: 979-8223088998

Written by Mazen Kaldas.

Unraveling the Secrets of Anti-Aging in the

Digital & AI World

Introduction:

Welcome to the fascinating world of anti-aging, where the boundaries of human lifespan and vitality are explored. Anti-aging, also known as rejuvenation or age reversal, is an emerging field that seeks to reverse or slow down the aging process, allowing individuals to enjoy a longer and healthier life. Powered by cutting-edge scientific research and innovative technologies, anti-aging aims to unravel the underlying mechanisms of aging, identify interventions to mitigate age-related damage, and restore youthful characteristics at a cellular, molecular, and systemic level. Through the convergence of disciplines such as genetics, regenerative medicine, and biomedical engineering, scientists are striving to unlock the secrets of longevity, pushing the boundaries of what it means to age and opening new possibilities for a future where aging is no longer an inevitable decline but a reversible and manageable process. Join us on this captivating journey as we explore the frontiers of anti-aging, where science and technology converge to reshape our understanding of lifespan and revolutionize the way we age.

Table of Content:

Chapter 1: The Dawn of Immortality

- Introduction to the concept of anti-aging and its historical significance.
- The intersection of technology and longevity: the birth of the digital revolution.

Chapter 2: Age-Defying Technologies

- Exploring cutting-edge technologies that contribute to anti-aging.
- Artificial intelligence, nanotechnology and genetic engineering: pioneers of digital rejuvenation.

Chapter 3: The Power of Data

- Unveiling the role of data in understanding the aging process.

- The advent of big data and its impact on anti-aging research.
- Bioinformatics and computational biology: deciphering the fountain of youth.

Chapter 4: Digital Health and Longevity

- Harnessing the potential of wearables, telemedicine, and personalized medicine.
- Health tracking apps and devices: empowering individuals in their anti-aging journey.
- The promise of virtual reality in mental and emotional well-being.

Chapter 5: Mind and Body: A Digital Symbiosis

- Exploring the connection between mental health, mindfulness, and aging.
- Cognitive training and brain-computer interfaces: unlocking the secrets of a youthful mind.
- The role of digital wellness platforms in holistic anti-aging approaches.

Chapter 6: The Social Impact of Immortality

- Ethical dilemmas and philosophical considerations surrounding anti-aging technologies.
- The digital divide and accessibility challenges in a world of extended lifespans.
- Redefining societal structures, relationships, and cultural norms in an ageless society.

Chapter 7: The Quest for Eternal Youth

- Investigating groundbreaking research in the field of rejuvenation biotechnology.
- Telomeres, senescence, and cellular reprogramming decoding the aging code.
- The race to find the ultimate anti-aging intervention.

Chapter 8: Digital Immortality: Transcending the Physical Realm

- Exploring the concept of consciousness uploading and mind uploading.
- Virtual reality, augmented reality, and the future of human existence.

- Challenges and controversies in the y pursuit of digital immortality.

Chapter 9: The Role of AI in the Quest for Anti-Aging

- AI-powered drug discovery and personalized medicine.
- Machine learning algorithms and predictive modeling in anti-aging research.
- The ethical implications of AI-driven decision-making in healthcare.

Chapter 10: Embracing Agelessness: A Digital Manifesto

- Embracing the digital age as a catalyst for a healthier, longer life.
- The importance of education, lifestyle choices, and mental resilience in anti-aging.
- Navigating the brave new world of anti-aging in the digital era.

Epilogue: Beyond the Horizon

- Speculating on the future of anti-aging and its impact on society.
- Embracing the possibilities of a digitally empowered and ageless future.

Chapter 1: The Dawn of Immortality

Introduction to the concept of anti-aging and its historical significance

Throughout history, the desire to slow down or even reverse the aging process has captivated the human imagination. The concept of anti-aging, or the pursuit of extending human lifespan and maintaining vitality, has been a prevalent theme in various cultures and civilizations. From ancient legends of mythical fountains of youth to the modern scientific advancements, the quest for anti-aging has evolved.

In ancient times, numerous civilizations sought to unlock the secrets of eternal youth. The Egyptians, for instance, practiced elaborate skincare routines and utilized natural ingredients, while ancient Chinese medicine explored herbal remedies and holistic approaches to enhance longevity. Across different cultures, longevity was often associated with wisdom, prosperity, and spiritual enlightenment.

As scientific knowledge advanced, the study of aging became more formalized. In the early 20th century, the field of gerontology emerged, focusing on the biological, psychological, and social aspects of aging. Scientists began to unravel the complex processes underlying the aging phenomenon, leading to groundbreaking discoveries and innovative theories.

The discovery of DNA and the unraveling of the genetic code in the 1950s and 1960s opened up new avenues of exploration. The idea that our genetic material held clues to the aging process sparked tremendous interest. Researchers began investigating the role of telomeres, the

protective caps on the ends of chromosomes, and their correlation with cellular aging.

In recent decades, the concept of anti-aging has gained momentum with advancements in various scientific disciplines. Bio gerontologists, geneticists, neuroscientists, and other specialists have converged to deepen our understanding of aging, exploring potential interventions, and proposing theories on extending healthy lifespan.

Today, the concept of anti-aging extends beyond simply prolonging life; it encompasses the maintenance of physical health, cognitive abilities, and overall well-being as we age. The focus has shifted toward healthy aging, emphasizing the importance of preventive measures, lifestyle interventions, and personalized strategies.

The field of anti-aging has also witnessed the integration of technology, with artificial intelligence (AI) playing an increasingly significant role. AI algorithms can process vast amounts of biological data, identify patterns, and predict outcomes, aiding in the development of personalized interventions, drug discovery, and understanding the complex mechanisms of aging.

The historical significance of the concept of anti-aging lies in its reflection of human aspirations and the pursuit of a better quality of life. It is a testament to our innate desire for longevity, vitality, and the preservation of youthfulness. As we delve deeper into the science of aging and leverage the power of AI, the quest for anti-aging continues to captivate the human spirit, offering hope and possibilities for a future where the impacts of aging can be mitigated, and the potential for a fulfilling and vibrant life can be realized.

The intersection of technology and longevity: the birth of the digital revolution

The convergence of technology and longevity has given rise to a groundbreaking era known as the digital revolution in the pursuit of extending human lifespan and promoting healthy aging. Advancements in various fields, including digital technologies, artificial intelligence, genomics, and bioinformatics, have revolutionized the way we approach longevity research and healthcare. In this section, we explore the intersection of technology and longevity, tracing the birth of the digital revolution and its transformative impact on the pursuit of extended healthspan.

The digital revolution in longevity research encompasses the integration of cutting-edge technologies into various aspects of healthcare and anti-aging interventions. Digital technologies have enabled the collection and analysis of vast amounts of health data, providing valuable insights into the aging process and age-related diseases. Wearable devices, connected sensors, and mobile health apps have become tools for continuous monitoring of vital signs, physical activity, sleep patterns, and other health metrics. These digital tools empower individuals to take an active role in their health management and provide healthcare professionals with valuable data for personalized interventions.

Artificial intelligence (AI) plays a central role in the digital revolution, leveraging machine learning algorithms to analyze massive datasets and extract meaningful patterns. AI-driven predictive models have the potential to identify risk factors for age-related diseases, predict disease progression, and personalize treatment plans. By integrating data from various sources, such as genomics, electronic health records, and lifestyle factors, AI algorithms can generate valuable insights to guide anti-aging interventions and promote individualized approaches to healthcare.

Genomics and bioinformatics have also become integral components of the digital revolution in longevity research. The mapping of the human genome has provided valuable insights into the genetic factors influencing the aging process. Bioinformatics, through computational analysis and interpretation of genomic data, helps uncover patterns, identify disease-associated genes, and explore potential therapeutic targets. The integration of genomics and bioinformatics with digital technologies allows for a more comprehensive understanding of the complex interactions between genes, environment, and aging, leading to the development of targeted interventions and personalized anti-aging strategies.

Moreover, the digital revolution has transformed healthcare delivery through telemedicine and virtual care. Remote consultations, digital health platforms, and telehealth services have become essential components of healthcare systems, facilitating access to medical expertise, reducing geographical barriers, and improving patient outcomes. This digital transformation allows individuals to receive healthcare services, including diagnosis, treatment, and preventive care, remotely, minimizing the need for physical visits to healthcare facilities.

The impact of the digital revolution in longevity extends beyond scientific research and healthcare delivery. It has also reshaped societal attitudes towards aging and well-being. The widespread availability of health information, online communities, and digital platforms for healthy living has empowered individuals to take charge of their aging process and actively seek strategies for healthy aging. The digital revolution has facilitated knowledge sharing, community building, and collaboration among researchers, healthcare professionals, and individuals passionate about extending healthspan and promoting well-being.

However, the digital revolution in longevity research also presents challenges and ethical considerations. Ensuring data privacy, security, and ethical use of personal health information is paramount. Addressing issues of data ownership, access disparities, and equity in the digital realm is crucial to avoid exacerbating existing healthcare inequalities. Ethical frameworks and regulatory policies need to keep pace with the rapid advancements in digital technologies to safeguard individual rights and protect vulnerable populations.

The intersection of technology and longevity has given birth to the digital revolution, revolutionizing the pursuit of extended healthspan and healthy aging. Through the integration of digital technologies, AI, genomics, and bioinformatics, the digital revolution offers unprecedented opportunities for understanding the aging process, developing personalized interventions, and transforming healthcare delivery.

Embracing the digital revolution in longevity research holds the potential to improve individual well-being, reshape societal attitudes towards aging, and usher in an era of extended healthspan and enhanced quality of life.

Chapter 2: Age-Defying Technologies

Exploring cutting-edge technologies that contribute to anti-aging

The pursuit of anti-aging has been propelled by a wave of cutting-edge technologies that hold immense promise for extending human health span and vitality. These innovative advancements span various fields, from genetics and regenerative medicine to artificial intelligence and nanotechnology. By harnessing these technologies, researchers are forging new paths towards understanding the aging process and developing interventions that may mitigate its effects. Let's explore some of the remarkable cutting-edge technologies contributing to anti-aging research.

Genomic Medicine:

Advancements in genomic medicine have revolutionized our understanding of aging. Through large-scale genetic studies and next-generation sequencing technologies, researchers can identify genetic factors associated with longevity and age-related diseases. This knowledge helps uncover potential targets for intervention and aids in the development of personalized anti-aging strategies.

Stem Cell and Regenerative Therapies:

Stem cell and regenerative therapies offer promising avenues for anti-aging research. Stem cells have the remarkable ability to differentiate into various cell types and replace damaged or aging cells. Researchers are exploring ways to harness the regenerative potential of stem cells to restore tissue function, repair organs, and rejuvenate the body.

Telomere Maintenance:

Telomeres, the protective caps at the ends of chromosomes, play a crucial role in cellular aging. Telomere shortening is associated with aging and age-related diseases. Scientists are investigating telomere maintenance mechanisms, including telomerase activation and other techniques, to potentially slow down telomere attrition and delay the aging process.

Senescence and Senolytics:

Cellular senescence, the irreversible arrest of cell division, is a hallmark of aging. Researchers are focusing on understanding senescence-associated processes and developing senolytic therapies that target and eliminate senescent cells. These interventions aim to rejuvenate tissues and alleviate age-related conditions associated with senescence.

Artificial Intelligence and Machine Learning:

Artificial intelligence and machine learning have emerged as powerful tools in anti-aging research. AI algorithms can analyze large-scale datasets, such as genomics, proteomics, and medical records, to identify patterns, biomarkers, and potential interventions. Machine learning enables the prediction of age-related risks, personalized medicine approaches, and the acceleration of drug discovery.

Nanotechnology:

Nanotechnology holds great potential for anti-aging interventions. Researchers are exploring the use of nanoparticles for targeted drug delivery, imaging, and regenerative purposes. Nanomaterials and Nano devices offer precise control at the nanoscale, enabling enhanced diagnostics, therapeutics, and tissue engineering approaches.

Bioinformatics and Data Integration:

Bioinformatics plays a critical role in anti-aging research, facilitating the analysis and integration of diverse biological data. The integration of genomics, proteomics, metabolomics, and other "omics" data provides a comprehensive view of the aging process, aiding in the identification of key pathways, biomarkers, and therapeutic targets.

These cutting-edge technologies collectively offer a multifaceted approach to anti-aging research. As they continue to evolve and synergize, researchers are gaining deeper insights into the mechanisms of aging and developing innovative interventions to promote healthy aging. While challenges remain, the convergence of these technologies holds tremendous promise for reshaping our understanding of aging, extending human health span, and realizing a future where age- related diseases are better managed, and the vitality of life is prolonged.

Artificial intelligence, nanotechnology and genetic engineering: pioneers of digital rejuvenation

Artificial intelligence (AI), nanotechnology, and genetic engineering are the pioneering forces behind the emerging field of digital rejuvenation. These cutting-edge technologies hold immense promise in the pursuit of reversing or slowing down the aging process. By combining their powers, researchers are pushing the boundaries of what is possible, paving the way for a future where digital interventions can rejuvenate and revitalize the human body.

Let's explore the role of AI, nanotechnology, and genetic engineering as pioneers of digital rejuvenation.

Artificial intelligence plays a pivotal role in digital rejuvenation by harnessing the power of data analysis, machine learning, and predictive modeling. AI algorithms can sift through vast amounts of biological data, including genomic information, proteomic profiles, and clinical records, to identify patterns, biomarkers, and potential interventions. Through AI-guided simulations, researchers can test the effects of various treatments and interventions on aging processes, leading to the discovery of innovative strategies for rejuvenation.

Nanotechnology offers unprecedented opportunities in digital rejuvenation by manipulating matter at the nanoscale. Researchers can engineer nanoparticles and Nano devices with remarkable precision, allowing for targeted drug delivery, cellular repair, and tissue regeneration. By leveraging nanotechnology, scientists can develop innovative approaches to rejuvenate cells, repair damaged tissues, and restore organ function. Nanoscale interventions hold the potential to reverse the aging process at its most fundamental level, enabling a new era of ageless vitality.

Genetic engineering is a transformative technology that allows researchers to modify and manipulate the genetic makeup of organisms. With the advent of CRISPR-Cas9 and other gene-editing tools, scientists can target specific genes and make precise modifications, offering the possibility of correcting genetic mutations associated with aging and age-related diseases. Genetic engineering opens up avenues for enhancing cellular repair mechanisms, extending telomeres, and promoting longevity-associated pathways. By fine-tuning the genetic blueprint, researchers aim to rejuvenate the body and unlock the secrets of sustained youthfulness.

Together, AI, nanotechnology, and genetic engineering are driving the frontiers of digital rejuvenation. These pioneering technologies are interwoven, with AI guiding the analysis and interpretation of complex biological data, nanotechnology delivering targeted interventions at the cellular level, and genetic engineering offering precise genetic modifications to optimize rejuvenation strategies. Their convergence offers unprecedented potential to revolutionize healthcare, enabling personalized, precise, and proactive interventions for healthy aging.

While the prospects of digital rejuvenation are exhilarating, ethical considerations, safety precautions, and responsible use of these technologies are of paramount importance. Striking a balance between scientific progress and ethical implications will be crucial as researchers navigate the uncharted territory of digital rejuvenation.

The trio of artificial intelligence, nanotechnology, and genetic engineering serves as the pioneering forces in digital rejuvenation. With their combined power, these technologies push the boundaries of scientific knowledge and open up possibilities for reversing or slowing down the aging process. As researchers continue to explore the synergistic potential of these fields, the future holds exciting prospects for achieving ageless vitality and redefining the limits of human longevity.

Chapter 3: The Power of Data

Unveiling the role of data in understanding the aging process

Unveiling the role of data is crucial in our quest to understand the intricacies of the aging process. With the advent of digital technologies and the exponential growth of data, researchers have gained unprecedented access to vast amounts of information related to aging, genetics, lifestyle, and health. By analyzing this wealth of data, scientists can uncover patterns, correlations, and predictive models that shed light on the underlying mechanisms of aging.

Through comprehensive data analysis, researchers can identify key factors that contribute to the aging process, including genetic variations, environmental influences, and lifestyle choices. The utilization of big data enables the identification of biomarkers of aging, age-related diseases, and the development of targeted interventions to delay or mitigate their effects.

Furthermore, data-driven research allows for personalized approaches to aging, taking into account individual variations and optimizing interventions based on specific genetic and lifestyle profiles.

Artificial intelligence (AI) plays a pivotal role in unraveling the complexities of the aging process, shedding light on its underlying mechanisms and providing valuable insights to researchers. By analyzing vast amounts of biological data, AI algorithms can identify patterns, correlations, and predictive markers associated with aging.

Genomic data, proteomics, metabolomics, and other biological information can be processed and integrated to develop a comprehensive understanding of aging at a molecular and systemic level. AI-powered computational models and simulations allow researchers to simulate the effects of various factors and interventions, enabling the exploration of potential anti-aging strategies. Moreover, AI assists in identifying key molecular targets, pathways, and cellular processes involved in aging, facilitating the discovery of novel therapeutic approaches.

By leveraging the power of AI, scientists can accelerate the pace of aging research, deepen our understanding of age-related diseases, and pave the way for the development of interventions that promote healthy aging and enhance human well-being. The unveiling of the role of data in understanding the aging process empowers researchers to delve deeper into the complexities of aging, driving advancements in anti-aging research and ultimately enhancing our ability to promote healthy aging and extend lifespan.

The advent of big data and its impact on anti-aging research

In recent years, the advent of big data has revolutionized various fields, including healthcare and anti-aging research. The availability of vast amounts of data,

coupled with advancements in computing power and data analytics, has transformed the way researchers approach the study of aging and the development of anti-aging interventions. In this section, we explore the impact of big data on anti-aging research and how it has opened up new avenues for understanding the aging process and promoting healthy aging.

Big data refers to large and complex datasets that are difficult to manage and analyze using traditional methods. In the context of anti-aging research, big data encompasses a wide range of information, including genomics data, electronic health records, imaging data, lifestyle data, and social determinants of health. These datasets provide researchers with a comprehensive view of an individual's health status, disease progression, and response to treatments. The analysis of big data allows for the identification of patterns, correlations, and trends that can uncover insights into the aging process and age-related diseases.

One of the significant impacts of big data on anti-aging research is the ability to conduct large-scale studies and generate more robust and reliable results. Traditionally, research studies were limited by sample sizes and resource constraints. However, with big data, researchers can access extensive datasets from diverse populations, enabling more comprehensive analyses and improving the generalizability of research findings. This expanded scope of research allows for a deeper understanding of the factors influencing the aging process and the identification of potential targets for intervention.

Furthermore, big data analytics facilitates the discovery of novel biomarkers, genetic associations, and therapeutic targets related to aging. By analyzing large datasets, researchers can identify genetic variants, epigenetic modifications, and other molecular signatures associated with healthy aging or age-related diseases. This knowledge can inform the development of targeted interventions and personalized anti-aging strategies. Additionally, big data analytics enables the identification of risk factors, predictive models, and early warning signs for age-related conditions, allowing for timely interventions and preventive measures.

The integration of big data in anti-aging research also opens up possibilities for precision medicine and personalized interventions. By analyzing individual-level data, including genomics, lifestyle factors, and health records, researchers can develop models that predict an individual's risk of developing specific age-related diseases or assess their response to particular treatments. This information enables the customization of interventions to an individual's unique needs, maximizing their chances of successful outcomes and reducing potential adverse effects.

Moreover, big data analytics fosters collaboration and data sharing among researchers and institutions. By aggregating and harmonizing data from multiple sources, researchers can pool resources, access larger datasets, and conduct more comprehensive analyses. Collaborative efforts and data sharing initiatives promote faster and more impactful discoveries in the field of anti-aging research, accelerating the development of innovative interventions and approaches.

Despite the numerous opportunities that big data brings to anti-aging research, challenges also exist. Ensuring data privacy and security is a critical consideration when dealing with large datasets containing sensitive health information. Compliance with legal and ethical standards, such as data anonymization and consent procedures, is paramount to protect individual privacy and maintain trust in the research process. Additionally, data quality, standardization, and interoperability pose challenges when integrating diverse datasets from various sources, requiring robust data management strategies and standardized protocols.

The advent of big data has transformed anti-aging research, offering unprecedented opportunities for understanding the aging process and developing effective interventions. By harnessing the power of large and complex datasets, researchers can uncover patterns, identify biomarkers, and personalize interventions to promote healthy aging. The utilization of big data in anti-aging research has the potential to unlock new insights, accelerate discoveries, and shape the future of healthcare by ushering in an era of personalized, data-driven approaches to aging and well-being.

Bioinformatics and computational biology: deciphering the fountain of youth

Bioinformatics and computational biology have emerged as indispensable disciplines in the quest to decipher the elusive "fountain of youth." By harnessing the power of data analysis, algorithms, and computational models, researchers are unraveling the intricate mechanisms underlying aging and paving the way for interventions that may slow down or reverse the aging process. Let's delve into the exciting world of bioinformatics and computational biology and explore their crucial role in the pursuit of prolonged youthfulness.

Bioinformatics, at its core, involves the application of computational tools and techniques to analyze vast amounts of biological data. Genomic sequences, proteomic profiles, metabolomics data, and clinical information are among the wealth of data sources bioinformaticians explore. These data provide critical insights into the molecular signatures, pathways, and regulatory mechanisms associated with aging and age-related diseases.

One of the primary goals of bioinformatics is to integrate and interpret these diverse datasets. By employing advanced algorithms, statistical methods, and machine learning approaches, bioinformaticians can uncover patterns, identify biomarkers, and predict age-related risks. For example, by analyzing genomic information, they can identify genetic variations that may influence the rate of aging or predispose individuals to certain age-related conditions.

In addition to data analysis, computational models play a vital role in understanding aging processes.

Through mathematical and computational frameworks, researchers can simulate aging-related phenomena, including cellular senescence, genetic interactions, and physiological changes. These models enable scientists to test hypotheses, predict outcomes, and explore potential interventions before embarking on time-consuming and costly experiments. The integration of bioinformatics and computational biology has also paved the way for personalized medicine approaches in anti-aging research. By combining genomic information, health records, lifestyle data, and computational algorithms, researchers can develop personalized interventions and therapeutic strategies tailored to an individual's unique genetic profile and risk factors. This personalized approach holds immense potential for optimizing anti-aging interventions and improving outcomes in the pursuit of prolonged health span.

Moreover, bioinformatics and computational biology are revolutionizing drug discovery and development. Virtual screening techniques, aided by AI algorithms, enable researchers to sift through vast chemical libraries to identify potential anti-aging compounds. Additionally, computational models can predict the effectiveness and safety of these compounds, narrowing down the search for promising candidates.

As bioinformatics and computational biology continue to evolve, the field faces both opportunities and challenges. The integration of multi-omics data, the development of more sophisticated algorithms, and the establishment of robust databases are crucial for enhancing our understanding of aging and uncovering the secrets of prolonged youthfulness. Ethical considerations, data privacy, and the interpretation of complex results also warrant careful attention.

Bioinformatics and computational biology are key drivers in the pursuit of unraveling the fountain of youth. These disciplines enable researchers to harness the power of data analysis, modeling, and prediction to delve into the intricate mechanisms of aging.

By deciphering the secrets hidden within the vast biological datasets, bioinformatics and computational biology hold the potential to guide us closer to interventions that may enhance health span, promote healthy aging, and unveil the path to a vibrant and enduring life.

Chapter 4: Digital Health and Longevity

Harnessing the potential of wearables, telemedicine, and personalized medicine

In the realm of healthcare and aging, the convergence of wearables, telemedicine, and personalized medicine has ushered in a new era of proactive and individualized care. These technologies are revolutionizing how we monitor health, deliver medical services remotely, and tailor interventions to meet the unique needs of each individual. Let's explore how wearables, telemedicine, and personalized medicine are shaping the future of healthcare.

Wearables, such as fitness trackers, smartwatches, and biosensors, have become ubiquitous tools for health monitoring. These devices can collect real-time data on vital signs, physical activity, sleep patterns, and more. Wearables empower individuals to take an active role in managing their health, providing them with valuable insights into their well-being and enabling early detection of potential health issues. Moreover, wearables allow for continuous monitoring, offering a more comprehensive and accurate picture of an individual's health status.

Telemedicine, fueled by advancements in communication technology, enables remote delivery of healthcare services. Through video consultations, remote monitoring, and digital health platforms, individuals can access medical expertise and receive personalized care regardless of their geographic location. Telemedicine eliminates barriers to healthcare access, particularly for those in remote areas or with limited mobility. It facilitates early intervention, reduces hospital visits, and enhances the efficiency of healthcare systems. Moreover, telemedicine allows healthcare providers to monitor patients remotely, ensuring timely interventions and facilitating proactive management of chronic conditions.

Personalized medicine takes into account an individual's unique genetic, environmental, and lifestyle factors to tailor medical interventions specifically to their needs. This approach moves away from the traditional "one-size-fits-all" model and considers the distinct characteristics of each individual. Advances in genomic sequencing, bioinformatics, and AI have paved the way for precision medicine. By analyzing an individual's genetic profile, healthcare providers can predict disease susceptibility, identify optimal treatments, and even assess an individual's response to specific medications. Personalized medicine empowers individuals by providing targeted interventions, minimizing adverse effects, and optimizing therapeutic outcomes.

The integration of wearables, telemedicine, and personalized medicine is transforming healthcare delivery and empowering individuals to actively manage their health throughout the aging process. By leveraging wearables, individuals can continuously monitor their health parameters, track progress, and make informed decisions about their lifestyle choices. Telemedicine expands access to specialized care, enables remote monitoring of chronic conditions, and facilitates timely interventions. The combination of wearables and telemedicine enables healthcare providers to gather real-time data, leading to personalized interventions and early detection of potential health issues.

Personalized medicine completes the trifecta by leveraging an individual's unique genetic profile to tailor treatments, optimize therapeutic outcomes, and pave the way for preventive strategies.

While these technologies hold immense potential, challenges must be addressed. Data security, privacy concerns, and the need for effective integration with healthcare systems are critical considerations. Additionally, equitable access to these technologies and addressing the digital divide are essential to ensure that these advancements benefit all individuals.

The harnessing of wearables, telemedicine, and personalized medicine has opened up a world of possibilities in healthcare and aging.

These technologies empower individuals to monitor and take charge of their health, enable remote access to specialized care, and provide personalized interventions based on individual characteristics. As technology continues to evolve, the potential to improve health outcomes, promote healthy aging, and enhance the overall well-being of individuals grows exponentially.

Health tracking apps and devices: empowering individuals in their anti-aging journey

Health tracking apps and devices have become integral tools in empowering individuals on their anti-aging journey. By providing valuable insights, personalized feedback, and continuous monitoring of health parameters, these technologies support proactive health management and facilitate the pursuit of a vibrant and age-defying lifestyle. In this section will explore how health tracking apps and devices are revolutionizing anti-aging strategies and empowering individuals to take control of their well-being. Health tracking apps and devices encompass a wide range of technologies, from smartphone applications to wearable devices and smart scales.

These tools allow individuals to monitor various aspects of their health, such as physical activity, heart rate, sleep quality, nutrition, and stress levels. By gathering and analyzing this data, individuals can gain a comprehensive understanding of their overall health and identify areas that may require attention or improvement one of the primary benefits of health tracking apps and devices is their ability to provide real-time feedback and personalized recommendations.

These technologies offer insights into an individual's progress towards health goals, provide actionable steps for improvement, and offer motivation and reminders to stay on track. Whether it's monitoring step counts, tracking calorie intake, or reminding individuals to practice mindfulness, these tools serve as constant companions on the path to healthy aging. Moreover, health tracking apps and devices facilitate self-awareness and promote healthy habits. By visualizing data trends and patterns over time, individuals can identify how lifestyle choices impact their health and make informed decisions to optimize well-being. For instance, individuals can adjust their exercise routines, modify their dietary choices, or adapt their sleep patterns based on the insights provided by these technologies.

This self-awareness empowers individuals to proactively address potential health issues, mitigate risks, and make positive changes that contribute to healthy aging. Another significant advantage of health tracking apps and devices is their ability to foster accountability and social support. Many of these technologies offer features that allow individuals to connect with friends, family, or online communities, sharing progress, challenges, and goals. This social aspect creates a supportive environment where individuals can seek encouragement, exchange tips, and engage in friendly competition, further motivating them to maintain a healthy lifestyle.

Additionally, the integration of health tracking apps and devices with other digital platforms, such as electronic health records or telemedicine systems, enables seamless communication between individuals and healthcare providers. By sharing health data in real-time, individuals can receive personalized recommendations, feedback, and remote monitoring from healthcare professionals.

This collaboration ensures that individuals receive timely interventions, tailored guidance, and ongoing support in their anti-aging journey. While health tracking apps and devices offer significant benefits, it's crucial to consider factors such as data privacy, accuracy of measurements, and the need for responsible use. It's essential for individuals to choose reputable and validated apps and devices and to understand the limitations of the data they provide.

Regular communication with healthcare providers remains vital to interpret and contextualize the information gathered through these technologies effectively. Health tracking apps and devices are powerful tools that empower individuals in their anti-aging journey. By providing personalized feedback, continuous monitoring, and actionable insights, these technologies enable individuals to take an active role in managing their health, optimizing well-being, and pursuing healthy aging.

As these technologies continue to evolve, the potential to enhance health outcomes, prevent age-related diseases, and promote lifelong vitality becomes increasingly accessible to individuals worldwide.

The promise of virtual reality in mental and emotional well-being

Virtual reality (VR) is rapidly emerging as a powerful tool with the potential to revolutionize mental and emotional well-being. By creating immersive and interactive simulated environments, VR opens up new possibilities for therapeutic interventions, self-exploration, and emotional healing. The promise of VR in enhancing mental and emotional well-being lies in its unique ability to transport individuals to alternative realities, providing a safe space for personal growth, exposure therapy, and the cultivation of positive emotions.

One area where VR shows great promise is in the treatment of mental health disorders. For individuals with anxiety, phobias, or post-traumatic stress disorder (PTSD), VR-based exposure therapy offers a controlled and realistic environment to confront and overcome their fears. By gradually exposing individuals to triggering situations in a virtual setting, therapists can guide them through the process of desensitization and reprogramming their responses. VR-based therapies can also be tailored to address specific mental health conditions, such as social anxiety or panic disorders, providing individuals with a safe and controlled space to practice coping strategies and build resilience.

Beyond specific therapeutic applications, VR has the potential to enhance emotional well-being through immersive experiences that foster relaxation, mindfulness, and stress reduction. VR environments can be designed to transport individuals to serene landscapes, tranquil natural settings, or serene meditation spaces, allowing them to escape from the stresses of everyday life and engage in immersive mindfulness practices. By engaging multiple senses and offering a sense of presence, VR can deepen the relaxation response, promote emotional regulation, and improve overall well-being.

Virtual reality also holds promise in promoting empathy, compassion, and emotional connection. VR experiences can simulate scenarios where individuals can embody different perspectives, allowing them to step into the shoes of others and gain a deeper understanding of diverse experiences. This immersive empathy-building can have transformative effects in promoting understanding, empathy, and compassion, ultimately enhancing social interactions and fostering emotional well-being.

Moreover, VR has the potential to address social isolation and loneliness, particularly among vulnerable populations. Through virtual social platforms, individuals can engage in meaningful interactions, connect with others, and participate in shared activities. This offers an avenue for combating social isolation, fostering a sense of belonging, and promoting emotional well-being.

While the promise of VR in mental and emotional well-being is vast, it is important to acknowledge the challenges and ethical considerations. Ensuring the safety and well-being of individuals during VR experiences, addressing potential adverse effects, and considering individual differences in susceptibility to VR-induced sensations are crucial areas of exploration.

Virtual reality holds tremendous promise in the realm of mental and emotional well-being. Its immersive and interactive nature offers innovative therapeutic interventions, relaxation techniques, and empathy-building experiences. As VR technologies continue to advance, with improved visual and auditory fidelity and more accessible hardware, the potential to transform mental health treatments, emotional well-being practices, and social connections becomes increasingly within reach.

The future holds exciting possibilities for harnessing the power of virtual reality to promote mental and emotional well-being, unlocking new dimensions of personal growth, healing, and emotional resilience.

Chapter 5: Mind and Body: A Digital Symbiosis

Exploring the connection between mental health, mindfulness, and aging

The connection between mental health, mindfulness, and aging is a subject of growing interest and importance. As individuals age, maintaining good mental health becomes paramount for overall well-being and quality of life. Mindfulness practices offer a powerful tool for nurturing mental health, reducing stress, and promoting emotional resilience. Let's delve into the intricate connection between mental health, mindfulness, and aging and explore how they intertwine to shape the aging experience.

Mental health plays a vital role in successful aging. Older adults may face unique challenges, such as chronic health conditions, loss of loved ones, or transitioning into retirement. These factors can contribute to increased stress, anxiety, and depression. Mental health disorders can significantly impact an individual's quality of life, cognitive function, and physical well-being. Therefore, fostering mental health is crucial in promoting healthy aging.

Mindfulness, rooted in ancient contemplative practices, offers a powerful approach to cultivating mental well-being. Mindfulness involves paying deliberate attention to the present moment, non-judgmentally, and with acceptance. Through mindfulness practices, individuals develop greater self-awareness, learn to regulate their emotions, and cultivate a compassionate attitude towards themselves and others. Regular mindfulness practice has been associated with reduced stress, improved emotional well-being, enhanced cognitive function, and better overall mental health.

The practice of mindfulness becomes particularly relevant in the context of aging. As individuals age, they may face increased vulnerability to stressors, cognitive changes, and emotional fluctuations. Mindfulness provides tools to navigate these challenges with resilience, fostering a sense of inner peace, acceptance, and gratitude. It allows individuals to focus on the present moment, savoring the positive aspects of their lives, and building emotional resilience to cope with the inevitable changes and losses that accompany aging.

Moreover, mindfulness practices have been shown to positively impact physical health outcomes. Regular mindfulness practice can lower blood pressure, reduce inflammation, improve sleep quality, and enhance immune system function. These physical health benefits contribute to overall well-being and support healthy aging.

The connection between mental health, mindfulness, and aging goes beyond individual well-being. Research suggests that mindfulness practices can also enhance interpersonal relationships and social connections, which are crucial factors in maintaining mental health and combating loneliness in older adults. By fostering empathy, compassion, and non-judgmental attitudes, mindfulness helps individuals build meaningful connections, strengthen social support networks, and promote a sense of belonging.

It is important to note that mindfulness is not a cure-all for mental health challenges associated with aging. While it offers valuable tools for promoting well-being, it should complement a comprehensive approach that includes appropriate mental health interventions, social support, and access to professional care when needed.

The connection between mental health, mindfulness, and aging is profound. Fostering mental well-being is essential for successful aging, and mindfulness practices offer a powerful approach to cultivating mental resilience, reducing stress, and enhancing overall well-being.

By integrating mindfulness into daily life, individuals can navigate the challenges of aging with greater clarity, compassion, and emotional balance. Mindfulness has the potential to transform the aging experience, promoting mental health, and fostering a sense of well-being throughout the journey of aging.

Cognitive training and brain-computer interfaces: unlocking the secrets of a youthful mind

Cognitive training and brain-computer interface (BCI) technologies are paving the way for unlocking the secrets of a youthful mind. As individuals age, maintaining cognitive abilities becomes increasingly important for overall well-being and quality of life. Cognitive training offers targeted exercises and interventions to improve cognitive function, while BCI technologies provide a direct interface between the brain and external devices, enabling new possibilities for cognitive enhancement. Let's explore how cognitive training and BCI are working in tandem to unlock the potential of a youthful mind.

Cognitive training involves engaging in specific activities and exercises designed to challenge and improve cognitive abilities. These programs often focus on areas such as memory, attention, problem-solving, and executive functions. Through structured training and practice, individuals can strengthen neural connections, improve cognitive processes, and enhance overall cognitive performance. Cognitive training programs can take various forms, including computer-based exercises, puzzles, gamified applications, and interactive tasks tailored to individual needs.

Cognitive training holds immense promise in promoting a youthful mind by harnessing the brain's neuroplasticity—the ability of the brain to adapt and rewire itself in response to new experiences. Research suggests that engaging in regular cognitive training can improve cognitive abilities, enhance memory, boost attention span, and increase information processing speed. These improvements can have significant implications for cognitive health and quality of life, allowing individuals to maintain independence, cognitive vitality, and a sense of mental sharpness as they age.

Brain-computer interface technologies take cognitive enhancement a step further by directly linking the human brain with external devices or computers. BCIs enable individuals to control devices or receive feedback based on their brain activity, bypassing traditional input methods such as touch or speech. BCIs can be used to develop assistive technologies, rehabilitation tools, and even enhance cognitive abilities.

One area where BCI technologies show promise is in neurofeedback training. Neurofeedback involves providing real-time feedback to individuals about their brain activity and enabling them to learn to regulate their brainwaves. By receiving immediate feedback, individuals can develop greater control over their brain activity and learn to modulate specific patterns associated with cognitive performance. This can result in improved attention, focus, and overall cognitive function.

BCIs can also be used in cognitive augmentation, where external devices or implants enhance cognitive abilities directly. For example, researchers are exploring the potential of brain implants to restore memory function in individuals with cognitive impairments. By directly stimulating specific brain regions or establishing neural interfaces, these technologies aim to enhance memory recall and overall cognitive performance.

The combination of cognitive training and BCI technologies offers a powerful synergy in unlocking the secrets of a youthful mind. By combining targeted cognitive exercises and interventions with direct brain-computer interfaces, individuals can potentially enhance cognitive abilities, restore functions, and tap into the full potential of their cognitive capabilities.

It is important to note that cognitive training and BCI technologies are still in the early stages of development, and further research is needed to fully understand their effectiveness, long-term implications, and potential risks. Ethical considerations, privacy concerns, and responsible use of these technologies are essential aspects that must be carefully addressed.

Cognitive training and brain-computer interface technologies hold great promise in unlocking the secrets of a youthful mind. By engaging in targeted cognitive exercises and utilizing direct brain-computer interfaces, individuals can enhance cognitive abilities, improve memory, and tap into the brain's potential for neuroplasticity.

As these technologies continue to advance and researchers delve deeper into their applications, the potential to unlock and maintain a youthful mind becomes increasingly within reach.

The role of digital wellness platforms in holistic anti-aging approaches

Digital wellness platforms are playing a crucial role in holistic anti-aging approaches, empowering individuals to take charge of their well-being across multiple dimensions. These platforms leverage technology and digital tools to provide comprehensive support, resources, and personalized interventions that address the physical, mental, emotional, and social aspects of aging. By combining advanced technologies with evidence-based strategies, digital wellness platforms are transforming the way individuals approach anti-aging, promoting holistic well-being and enhancing the overall quality of life.

One of the primary advantages of digital wellness platforms is their ability to provide accessible and convenient resources for individuals to manage their well-being. These platforms offer a wide range of features, such as fitness tracking, nutrition planning, stress reduction techniques, sleep monitoring, and mindfulness practices. Through user-friendly interfaces and mobile applications, individuals can easily access these tools and integrate them into their daily routines, fostering long-term behavior change and self-care.

Digital wellness platforms also facilitate personalized interventions tailored to individual needs and goals. By leveraging data analytics, artificial intelligence, and machine learning algorithms, these platforms can gather and interpret user data to provide customized recommendations, insights, and feedback. For example, based on an individual's fitness level, preferences, and health profile, the platform may offer personalized workout routines, nutrition plans, and wellness practices that specifically target their unique needs. This personalization enhances engagement and motivation, ensuring that individuals receive interventions that resonate with their specific circumstances.

Digital wellness platforms promote holistic well-being by addressing mental and emotional health alongside physical fitness. These platforms often include features for stress management, mindfulness exercises, mood tracking, and even virtual coaching or therapy sessions. By integrating mental health support, individuals can cultivate emotional resilience, manage stress, and enhance overall psychological well-being. This holistic approach recognizes the interconnectedness of mind and body, highlighting the importance of mental and emotional well-being in the anti-aging journey.

Digital wellness platforms also foster social connectivity and community engagement, combating social isolation and promoting a sense of belonging. Many platforms include social features, allowing individuals to connect with like-minded individuals, participate in challenges, and share their progress. This virtual community aspect creates a supportive environment where individuals can find encouragement, accountability, and inspiration in their anti-aging journey. The power of social connection cannot be understated, as it contributes to overall well-being and enhances the motivation to sustain healthy habits.

As with any technology, the ethical considerations of digital wellness platforms should be carefully addressed. Ensuring data privacy, transparency in data collection and usage, and safeguarding against potential risks are critical aspects to be taken into account. Additionally, it is important to recognize that digital wellness platforms should complement, rather than replace, professional healthcare services. They should be utilized as supportive tools within a comprehensive healthcare approach.

Digital wellness platforms have emerged as valuable allies in holistic anti-aging approaches. By leveraging technology, data analytics, and personalized interventions, these platforms empower individuals to optimize their physical, mental, and emotional well-being.

By offering comprehensive support, fostering social connectivity, and integrating personalized interventions, digital wellness platforms promote holistic anti-aging approaches that enhance the overall quality of life and support individuals in their journey towards healthy and vibrant aging.

Chapter 6: The Social Impact of Immortality

Ethical dilemmas and philosophical considerations surrounding anti-aging technologies

The development and implementation of anti-aging technologies present a complex ethical dilemma and raise profound philosophical considerations. While these technologies hold the promise of extending human health span and mitigating age-related diseases, they also give rise to ethical questions related to fairness, access, the meaning of life, and the nature of human existence. Let's explore some of the key ethical and philosophical issues surrounding anti-aging technologies.

One of the fundamental ethical concerns is the question of equity and access. As anti-aging technologies advance, there is a risk that they may exacerbate existing social inequalities. If these interventions are primarily available to the wealthy and privileged, it could lead to a scenario where only a select few can access the benefits of prolonged health and vitality. This raises questions of fairness and social justice, as the disparity in access to anti-aging technologies could deepen existing disparities in health outcomes and quality of life.

Another ethical consideration is the potential for unintended consequences. While anti-aging technologies aim to enhance well-being and extend healthy lifespan, their long-term effects on individuals and society remain uncertain. It is crucial to carefully assess the potential risks, side effects, and unforeseen consequences of these interventions. Ethical frameworks should guide the responsible development and implementation of these technologies, ensuring that the benefits outweigh the risks and that individuals are adequately informed and protected.

Furthermore, the pursuit of anti-aging technologies prompts philosophical reflections on the nature of human existence and the meaning of life. Aging is a natural part of the human experience, intimately tied to the cycle of life, growth, and eventual decline. Anti-aging technologies challenge the notion of accepting the inevitability of aging and provoke discussions about what it means to be human. Some argue that aging contributes to the richness of human experience, providing opportunities for personal growth, wisdom, and the appreciation of life's transient nature. Opponents of anti-aging technologies argue that seeking to prolong life indefinitely detracts from the inherent value of the finite human experience.

Additionally, the desire to extend life raises ethical questions surrounding resource allocation and the potential strain on healthcare systems. If anti-aging technologies become widely accessible, the demand for healthcare services may increase exponentially, placing a burden on healthcare resources. Ethical considerations must be taken into account to ensure that the pursuit of anti-aging does not compromise the availability and quality of healthcare for other essential medical needs or marginalized populations.

Another ethical dilemma arises from the potential shift in societal structures and norms. Prolonged health span and life extension may disrupt established social institutions, such as retirement, family structures, and workforce dynamics. The implications of extended lifespans on intergenerational relationships, employment, and social contributions need careful consideration to ensure that the benefits of anti-aging technologies align with a thriving and equitable society.

Navigating the ethical and philosophical considerations surrounding anti-aging technologies requires a comprehensive approach that incorporates multidisciplinary perspectives, public engagement, and ethical frameworks. Open and transparent dialogue is essential to address these complex issues and ensure that the development and implementation of anti-aging technologies align with societal values and foster the well-being of all individuals.

The development of anti-aging technologies presents a profound ethical dilemma and prompts philosophical reflections on the nature of human existence, fairness, and societal implications.

While these technologies offer the potential for extended health span and improved quality of life, ethical considerations regarding equity, unintended consequences, the meaning of life, and resource allocation must be carefully examined. Balancing the pursuit of anti-aging technologies with ethical frameworks and societal values is crucial to navigate the ethical challenges and ensure that these advancements align with the collective well-being of individuals and society as a whole.

The digital divide and accessibility challenges in a world of extended lifespans

In a world of extended lifespans, the digital divide and accessibility challenges take on new significance. As anti-aging technologies advance and the potential for prolonged healthspan increases, it becomes crucial to address the disparities in digital access, technological literacy, and inclusive design. Ensuring equitable access to information, healthcare services, and digital resources becomes paramount to prevent the exacerbation of social inequalities. Let's explore the digital divide and accessibility challenges in the context of extended lifespans.

The digital divide refers to the gap between those who have access to digital technologies and those who do not. This gap encompasses disparities in internet access, computer literacy, and the ability to utilize digital resources effectively. In a world where anti-aging technologies and health information are increasingly digitized, the digital divide can significantly impact individuals' ability to access and benefit from these advancements. Those without access to digital technologies or the skills to navigate them may face barriers in receiving timely and relevant health information, engaging in telemedicine services, or accessing resources that promote healthy aging.

Accessibility challenges are another critical consideration. Extended lifespans raise the importance of inclusive design and accessibility measures in technology and digital platforms. As individuals age, they may experience physical, sensory, or cognitive impairments that affect their ability to access and use digital technologies. Ensuring that websites, applications, and digital content are accessible to individuals with disabilities becomes essential. Features such as text-to-speech functionality, large fonts, intuitive navigation, and alternative input methods can enhance accessibility and enable individuals of all ages to benefit from anti-aging technologies and digital resources.

Moreover, the accessibility challenges extend beyond the technological aspect. Language barriers, cultural factors, and varying levels of technological literacy also contribute to the digital divide and limit access to extended lifespan resources. Tailoring digital content and interventions to diverse populations, considering cultural nuances, and providing multilingual support are crucial steps towards inclusive access and effective utilization of anti-aging technologies.

Addressing the digital divide and accessibility challenges requires a multifaceted approach. Governments, policymakers, and organizations must prioritize bridging the digital divide by investing in infrastructure development, expanding internet access, and providing digital literacy programs. Additionally, initiatives to enhance accessibility in technology design, digital content creation, and healthcare services should be implemented to ensure that anti-aging resources are accessible to individuals of all ages, abilities, and socioeconomic backgrounds.

Collaboration between public and private sectors is essential in addressing the digital divide and accessibility challenges. Partnerships can foster the development of inclusive technologies, promote digital literacy initiatives,

and improve access to healthcare services through telemedicine and virtual platforms. By working together, stakeholders can reduce disparities, empower individuals, and ensure that extended lifespan resources are accessible to all.

It is important to note that addressing the digital divide and accessibility challenges is an ongoing process that requires continuous monitoring, evaluation, and adaptation. As technology evolves and anti-aging interventions advance, efforts to bridge the gap and promote accessibility should keep pace to avoid leaving vulnerable populations behind.

The digital divide and accessibility challenges present significant hurdles in a world of extended lifespans. Bridging the divide and ensuring access to anti-aging technologies, health information, and digital resources is crucial for promoting equitable and inclusive access to extended lifespan benefits. By addressing the digital divide, enhancing accessibility measures, and promoting digital literacy, society can empower individuals of all ages and backgrounds to fully participate in the opportunities offered by extended lifespans, fostering a more inclusive and thriving future for all.

Redefining societal structures, relationships, and cultural norms in an ageless society

In an ageless society, where extended lifespans and advancements in anti-aging technologies become a reality, redefining societal structures, relationships, and cultural norms becomes a crucial consideration. The transformative potential of prolonged health span and life extension challenges existing social institutions and prompts a reevaluation of traditional notions of aging, retirement, intergenerational dynamics, and the meaning of life. Let's explore the key aspects of societal redefinition in an ageless society.

One of the fundamental shifts in an ageless society is the redefinition of chronological age as a determinant of life stages and societal roles. Traditional age-based milestones, such as retirement or career progression, may need to be reassessed or redesigned to accommodate longer lifespans. The concept of a fixed retirement age may become obsolete, giving way to more flexible approaches that consider individual capabilities, personal aspirations, and contributions to society. This redefinition of life stages has implications for workforce dynamics, social security systems, and intergenerational relationships.

Interactions between generations also undergo transformation in an ageless society. The coexistence of individuals of varying ages and health statuses challenges the traditional generational divide and necessitates a reimagining of intergenerational relationships.

Age diversity can foster rich exchanges of knowledge, experiences, and perspectives, promoting mutual learning and appreciation.

Embracing intergenerational collaboration and fostering environments that facilitate the exchange of wisdom and skills can lead to stronger and more cohesive communities.

Cultural norms surrounding aging, beauty standards, and societal expectations may also evolve in an ageless society. Prevailing notions of youthfulness and beauty may be redefined to encompass a broader range of ages and appearances. This shift can promote a more inclusive and diverse understanding of beauty, challenge ageist attitudes, and foster a culture that values wisdom, experience, and vitality across the lifespan. Society may also reevaluate its emphasis on productivity and achievement, recognizing the importance of personal growth, well-being, and purposeful engagement beyond traditional metrics of success.

Moreover, an ageless society presents opportunities to redefine notions of personal identity and self-actualization. With extended lifespans, individuals have more time to explore new passions, pursue multiple careers, engage in lifelong learning, and embark on personal growth journeys. This can lead to a reimagining of personal fulfillment and purpose, shifting the focus from achieving specific milestones by a certain age to continuous self-discovery, development, and contribution to society.

In the context of family structures, an ageless society may see a reconfiguration of intergenerational support systems and caregiving roles. With increased lifespans, individuals may have the opportunity to play active roles as caregivers for older and younger family members simultaneously.

This calls for a reevaluation of caregiving policies, community support mechanisms, and the redistribution of caregiving responsibilities to ensure the wellbeing of all generations.

Redefining societal structures, relationships, and cultural norms in an ageless society requires a collective effort. It involves engaging in open and inclusive dialogues, promoting intergenerational collaboration, and considering diverse perspectives in policy development and decision-making processes.

Balancing individual aspirations, societal needs, and ethical considerations is crucial to foster a thriving and equitable society that embraces the opportunities and challenges of extended lifespans.

An ageless society necessitates the redefinition of societal structures, relationships, and cultural norms. By reconsidering traditional age-based milestones, fostering intergenerational collaboration, reimagining personal fulfillment, and challenging ageist attitudes, society can embrace the transformative potential of extended lifespans.

Redefining societal norms in an ageless society requires an inclusive and forward-thinking approach that promotes well-being, inclusivity, and the meaningful engagement of individuals of all ages, fostering a society that celebrates the richness and diversity of the human lifespan.

Chapter 7: The Quest for Eternal Youth

Investigating groundbreaking research in the field of rejuvenation biotechnology

Rejuvenation biotechnology is a rapidly advancing field that aims to reverse or slow down the aging process, promoting prolonged health span and vitality. Researchers around the world are pushing the boundaries of scientific knowledge, exploring innovative approaches to rejuvenation at the cellular and molecular levels.

One area of groundbreaking research in rejuvenation biotechnology revolves around cellular senescence-the state in which cells lose their ability to divide and function optimally.

Scientists are investigating ways to remove or rejuvenate senescent cells, as their accumulation has been linked to age-related diseases and the overall aging process.

Emerging therapies, such as senolytics and senomorphic drugs, target and eliminate these senescent cells or modulate their harmful

effects. Animal studies have shown promising results, with improvements in tissue function, increased lifespan, and delayed onset of age-related conditions. Human clinical trials are underway, opening up possibilities for targeted interventions to rejuvenate tissues and organs.

Another groundbreaking area of research focuses on regenerative medicine and stem cell therapies. Stem cells possess the unique ability, to self-renew and differentiate into various cell types, making them a valuable tool in rejuvenation biotechnology. Scientists are exploring methods to harness the potential of stem cells for tissue regeneration and repair.

This includes techniques to reprogram cells, such as induced pluripotent stem cells (iPSCs), which can be derived from adult cells and directed to differentiate into different cell types. IPSCs hold promise in regenerating damaged tissues and organs, potentially reversing age-related degeneration.

The field of epigenetics, which studies modifications to gene expression patterns without changing the underlying DNA sequence, has also seen groundbreaking advancements in v rejuvenation biotechnology. Researchers are investigating the manipulation of epigenetic marks to reverse age-associated changes in gene expression. By reprogramming epigenetic patterns, scientists aim to restore youthful cellular functions and promote healthy aging.

Epigenetic editing tools, such as CRISPR-based technologies, offer precise control over gene expression and hold the potential for targeted interventions to rejuvenate cells and tissues.

Furthermore, the exploration of caloric restriction mimetics and pharmacological interventions to mimic the beneficial effects of dietary restriction is an area of intense research.

Caloric restriction has been shown to extend lifespan and improve health span in various organisms. Scientists are now searching for compounds that can mimic the metabolic effects of caloric restriction without the need for extreme dietary changes. These caloric restriction mimetics aim to activate longevity-promoting pathways, such as sirtuins and AMP-activated protein kinase (AMPK), to promote cellular health and slow down the aging process.

Advancements in rejuvenation biotechnology also extend to the field of artificial intelligence (AI). AI-based approaches are being utilized to analyze complex biological data, identify patterns, and predict potential rejuvenation interventions. Machine learning algorithms can sift through vast amounts of information, including genomics, proteomics, and clinical data, to uncover novel targets and therapeutic strategies. AI-guided simulations and virtual screening methods are also aiding in the discovery of potential anti-aging compounds and drug candidates, accelerating the development of rejuvenation therapies.

While the progress in rejuvenation biotechnology is exciting, it is important to acknowledge the ethical considerations and potential challenges that come with these advancements. Responsible development, rigorous safety testing, equitable access, and consideration of the long-term effects on individuals and society are crucial aspects that need to be addressed.

Groundbreaking research in the field of rejuvenation biotechnology is revolutionizing our understanding of aging and opening up possibilities for prolonging health span and vitality. Investigating cellular senescence, regenerative medicine, epigenetics, caloric restriction mimetics, and the integration of AI are among the key areas driving advancements in this field. As research continues to progress, the potential for targeted interventions to reverse the aging process and promote healthy aging becomes increasingly within reach.

These groundbreaking discoveries hold immense promise in reshaping the landscape of aging, offering hope for a future where individuals can enjoy extended health and vitality throughout their lives.

Telomeres, senescence, and cellular reprogramming decoding the aging code

Telomeres, senescence, and cellular reprogramming are intricately linked factors that play a crucial role in the aging process. Understanding these components is vital for unraveling the mechanisms behind aging and potentially unlocking strategies to slow down or reverse it. Telomeres are protective caps at the ends of chromosomes that safeguard the integrity of DNA during cell division. They consist of repetitive DNA sequences and associated proteins that prevent the loss of genetic information. Telomeres naturally shorten with each round of cell division due to the "end replication problem," where the DNA replication machinery fails to replicate the very ends of chromosomes completely. Eventually, this shortening triggers cellular senescence- state in which cells lose their ability to divide and function optimally.

Senescence is a cellular response to various stressors, including telomere shortening, DNA damage, or other factors that can compromise cell integrity. Senescent cells exhibit distinct characteristics, such as altered gene expression, secretion of inflammatory molecules, and a senescence-associated secretory phenotype (SASP).

While cellular senescence initially serves as a protective mechanism to prevent damaged cells from proliferating, the accumulation of senescent cells over time contributes to tissue dysfunction, chronic inflammation, and age-related diseases.

Cellular reprogramming offers an intriguing approach to reverse or rejuvenate cells. It involves inducing pluripotency in adult cells, essentially converting them back to an embryonic-like state with the potential to differentiate into any cell type. This reprogramming is typically achieved through the introduction of key transcription factors, such as Oct4, Sox2, KIf4, and c-Myc. Reprogrammed cells, known as induced pluripotent stem cells (iPSCs), exhibit restored telomere length, restored gene expression patterns, and restored proliferative capacity. This process holds promise for regenerative medicine, as iPSCs can potentially be differentiated into any cell type to replace damaged or aged cells in tissues and organs.

Decoding the aging code requires a comprehensive understanding of how telomeres, senescence, and cellular reprogramming interact.

Telomere shortening is considered a hallmark of cellular aging, as it gradually leads to the accumulation of senescent cells. However, cellular reprogramming has demonstrated the ability to reverse age-associated changes in cells, rejuvenating them and resetting their telomere length. This raises the exciting possibility of using cellular reprogramming techniques to reverse aging at the cellular lever and potentially restore tissue and organ function.

Despite the promise of telomeres, senescence, and cellular reprogramming, challenges remain. For instance, fully understanding the precise mechanisms that govern telomere maintenance, senescence induction, and the reprogramming process is a complex task that requires further investigation. Ensuring the safety and efficacy of cellular reprogramming approaches is another important consideration. Researchers must address the potential risks of tumorigenesis or uncontrolled cell growth associated with reprogramming techniques.

Moreover, ethical considerations come into play when discussing the application of cellular reprogramming in humans. Issues such as the sourcing of cells, consent, and equitable access to potential rejuvenation therapies require careful attention and consideration.

Telomeres, senescence, and cellular reprogramming hold key roles in deciphering the aging code.

Understanding the dynamics between telomere length, cellular senescence, and the rejuvenating potential of cellular reprogramming offers invaluable insights into the aging process. By unraveling the intricacies of these components, researchers are advancing our knowledge and paving

the way for potential interventions to slow down or reverse aging, ultimately bringing us closer to the goal of promoting extended health span and improved quality of life.

The race to find the ultimate anti-aging intervention

The pursuit of the ultimate anti-aging intervention has sparked a global race among scientists, researchers, and pharmaceutical companies. With the goal of extending health span, improving quality of life, and potentially even reversing the aging process, this race represents a quest to unlock the secrets of longevity and rejuvenation.

One avenue of research focuses on understanding the underlying mechanisms of aging at the cellular and molecular levels. Scientists are investigating various hallmarks of aging, such as genomic instability, telomere attrition, epigenetic alterations, mitochondrial dysfunction, and cellular senescence. By deciphering the intricacies of these processes, researchers aim to identify key targets for intervention and develop therapies that can slow down or reverse age-related decline.

Another area of exploration involves harnessing the potential of regenerative medicine and stem cell therapies. Researchers are investigating the use of stem cells to repair and rejuvenate damaged tissues and organs. Stem cells possess the remarkable ability to self-renew and differentiate into different cell types, making them a valuable tool in the pursuit of anti-aging interventions. By leveraging the regenerative capacity of stem cells, scientists aim to replace or repair aged or damaged cells, potentially restoring tissue and organ function and reversing the effects of aging.

The race to find the ultimate anti-aging intervention also includes efforts to identify and develop pharmacological compounds that can slow down the aging process and enhance health span. Researchers are exploring a range of potential interventions, including caloric restriction mimetics, senolytics, and compounds that target age-related pathways such as m TOR, AMPK, and sirtuins. These interventions aim to modulate cellular metabolism, enhance stress resistance, and promote cellular and tissue health. In recent years, the field of artificial intelligence (AI) has also emerged as a valuable tool in the race to find the ultimate anti-aging intervention.

AI algorithms can analyze vast amounts of biological data, identify patterns, and predict potential interventions. Machine learning models aid in drug discovery, identifying novel targets, and designing optimized therapeutic approaches. AI-guided simulations and virtual screening methods accelerate the search for potential anti-aging compounds, streamlining the process and bringing us closer to effective interventions.

Collaboration and knowledge-sharing play a vital role in the race to find the ultimate anti-aging intervention. Researchers worldwide are increasingly collaborating to pool their expertise and resources, forming interdisciplinary teams to tackle the complex challenges associated with aging. Open-access databases, scientific conferences, and publications foster the exchange of ideas and accelerate progress in the field.

However, the pursuit of the ultimate anti-aging intervention also faces challenges and ethical considerations. Rigorous testing and safety evaluation are crucial to ensure the efficacy and safety of potential interventions. Ethical questions arise concerning equitable access to anti-aging interventions, the potential exacerbation of societal inequalities, and the impacts on social structures and healthcare systems. In conclusion, the race to find the ultimate anti-aging intervention represents a global effort to unlock the secrets of longevity and rejuvenation.

Scientists, researchers, and pharmaceutical companies are pushing the boundaries of knowledge and technology to develop interventions that can slow down or reverse the aging process, extend health span, and improve quality of life.

By leveraging advancements in cellular and molecular biology, regenerative medicine, pharmacology, and AI, the pursuit of the ultimate anti-aging intervention is bringing us closer to a future where age-related decline may be mitigated, and individuals can enjoy extended health and vitality throughout their lives.

Chapter 8: Digital Immortality: Transcending the Physical Realm

Exploring the concept of consciousness uploading and mind uploading

Consciousness uploading, also known as mind uploading or whole brain emulation, is a captivating concept that has gained attention in science fiction and philosophical discussions. It refers to the hypothetical process of transferring the contents of a person's mind, including their memories, personality, and subjective experiences, into a digital or artificial substrate.

This concept raises intriguing questions about the nature of consciousness, identity, and the potential for transcending biological limitations.

At its core, consciousness uploading is based on the idea that the mind is an information-processing system, and if that system can be replicated or transferred to a different substrate, the individual's consciousness could continue to exist in the new medium. Proponents of consciousness uploading argue that it could offer a means to overcome mortality, allowing individuals to exist beyond the lifespan of their biological bodies.

The process of consciousness uploading is often portrayed as a step-by-step transfer of the individual's neural patterns and connections into a digital or artificial system. This might involve scanning and mapping the structure and activity of the brain, capturing the intricate details that give rise to consciousness. The data would then be used to create a digital replica or simulation of the individual's mind, which could theoretically continue to exist and experience subjective consciousness.

One of the fascinating aspects of consciousness uploading is the potential for enhancing and modifying one's mind beyond its original biological form. Digital substrates could offer the possibility of augmenting cognitive abilities, expanding memory capacity, or even experiencing new forms of sensory perception.

This concept opens up possibilities for personal growth, exploration, and the ability to customize one's subjective experience in ways that were previously unimaginable. However, consciousness uploading also raises significant philosophical and ethical questions Critics argue that even if a digital replica of a person's mind is created, it may not truly represent the subjective experience and continuity of the original consciousness. They question whether the essence of subjective experience can truly be captured and transferred in a digital form, or if it is an emergent property of the physical brain. The concept of personal identity and whether a digital replica would retain the same sense of self, memories, and continuity also come into play.

Moreover, the ethical considerations surrounding consciousness uploading are substantial. Questions arise regarding the consent and rights of the individuals involved, as well as potential risks and unintended consequences. The creation and manipulation of digital consciousness raise concerns about privacy, control, and the potential for exploitation or manipulation of uploaded individuals.

It is important to note that the concept of consciousness uploading remains speculative and theoretical at present.

The technological advancements required to achieve such a feat are far beyond our current capabilities. While scientists continue to make progress in understanding the brain and developing technologies to interface with neural systems, consciousness and subjective experience remain complex and elusive phenomena that defy a complete understanding.

Exploring the concept of consciousness uploading and mind uploading raises thought-provoking questions about the nature of consciousness, personal identity, and the potential for transcending biological limitations.

While it captivates our imagination and fuels philosophical debates, the concept remains in the realm of speculation and poses significant ethical and philosophical challenges.

The exploration of consciousness uploading invites us to reflect on the nature of our existence and the possibilities that technology may hold for the future of human consciousness.

Virtual reality, augmented reality, and the future of human existence

Virtual reality (VR) and augmented reality (AR) technologies have transformed the way we perceive and interact with our digital and physical worlds. As these immersive technologies continue to advance, they hold the potential to reshape human existence in profound ways.

Virtual reality refers to the creation of a fully immersive digital environment that simulates real or imagined experiences. By wearing a VR headset and using motion-tracking devices, individuals can be transported to virtual worlds and interact with them in ways that mimic real-life experiences. From gaming and entertainment to education and training, VR offers a range of applications that enhance engagement, immersion, and presence.

Augmented reality, on the other hand, overlays digital information onto the physical world, blending the virtual and real. Through AR devices like smartphones, smart glasses, or headsets, users can see and interact with digital elements integrated into their immediate surroundings. AR has found applications in areas such as gaming, navigation, healthcare, retail, and industrial training, augmenting real-world experiences with contextual information and interactive digital content.

The convergence of VR and AR technologies has the potential to revolutionize human existence in multiple domains. In education, immersive VR experiences can transport students to historical events, distant planets, or complex scientific phenomena, providing engaging and interactive learning opportunities. AR can enhance the learning process by overlaying educational content onto real-world objects, enabling students to visualize and interact with abstract concepts.

In healthcare, VR and AR can be utilized for medical training, allowing students and professionals to practice surgeries or simulate challenging

medical scenarios in a safe and controlled environment. VR can also facilitate pain management, distraction techniques, or exposure therapy for phobias and anxiety disorders. AR applications can assist surgeons during complex procedures by overlaying patient data or real-time imaging directly onto their field of view.

Within the workplace, VR and AR technologies offer new possibilities for remote collaboration, training, and design. Virtual meetings conducted in immersive VR environments can bridge geographical distances and foster more effective communication and collaboration among teams. AR can provide real-time guidance and information to workers, reducing errors and enhancing productivity in fields such as manufacturing, logistics, and maintenance.

The impact of VR and AR extends beyond specific industries. These technologies have the potential to redefine social interactions, entertainment, and even the concept of reality itself. Virtual social platforms allow people from around the world to connect, interact, and share experiences in shared virtual spaces. VR concerts, gaming experiences, and immersive storytelling create new avenues for entertainment, blurring the boundaries between the physical and digital worlds.

As VR and AR technologies continue to evolve, the future holds even more transformative possibilities. Advancements in haptic feedback, brain-computer interfaces, and sensory stimulation can further enhance immersion and presence, allowing users to experience a broader range of sensations within virtual environments.

The concept of a metaverse -a persistent and shared virtual universe - has gained traction, envisioning a future where people live, work, and socialize in immersive virtual spaces.

While the potential benefits of VR, AR, and their convergence are vast, ethical considerations must accompany their development and integration into society. Questions related to privacy, security, addiction, and the blurring of real and virtual experiences need careful consideration to ensure responsible and beneficial deployment of these technologies.

Virtual reality, augmented reality, and their convergence hold immense potential to transform human existence across various domains. From education and healthcare to workplace collaboration and entertainment, these technologies enable immersive and interactive experiences that enhance learning, productivity, and social interactions. As these technologies advance, it is crucial to navigate their integration ethically and responsibly, ensuring that they serve as tools for human betterment and contribute positively to the future of our existence.

Challenges and controversies in the pursuit of digital immortality

The pursuit of digital immortality, the idea of preserving one's consciousness or mind in a digital or artificial form, raises significant challenges and controversies. While the concept captivates the imagination and offers potential solutions to the limitations of human mortality, it also presents complex ethical, philosophical, and technical considerations. In this page, we explore some of the challenges and controversies surrounding the pursuit of digital immortality.

One of the foremost challenges is the nature of consciousness itself. Consciousness is a deeply intricate and mysterious phenomenon, and its essence and subjective experience are still not fully understood. The concept of transferring consciousness into a digital or artificial substrate assumes that subjective experience can be replicated or transferred. However, the nature of subjective experience and the continuity of personal identity in a digital form remain open questions. Debates about the relationship between mind and body, the role of the physical brain in consciousness, and the potential loss of the embodied human experience emerge in discussions surrounding digital immortality. The technical challenges associated with achieving digital immortality are also substantial.

The brain is an incredibly complex organ, and mapping its intricate neural connections and activities with sufficient detail is currently beyond our capabilities. The creation of an accurate and comprehensive digital replica of an individual's mind is a formidable task that

requires advances in neuroscience, computational power, and data storage. Additionally, the computational resources needed to simulate and sustain a digital consciousness at a level of complexity equivalent to the human brain are currently beyond reach.

Ethical concerns and controversies surround the pursuit of digital immortality as well. Questions arise regarding the consent and rights of the individuals involved in the process. Ethical considerations extend to issues of privacy, control, and the potential for exploitation or manipulation of digital replicas or simulated consciousness. The creation of digital beings that possess consciousness or subjective experiences also raises moral questions about their treatment, rights, and responsibilities within society.

Moreover, the pursuit of digital immortality raises profound philosophical questions about the meaning and value of life. Critics argue that the finitude of life and the knowledge of mortality contribute to the richness and appreciation of human existence. Seeking to extend life indefinitely or to replicate consciousness in a digital form may detract from the inherent value of the finite human experience. Philosophical debates also revolve around the potential impact of digital immortality on concepts such as personal growth, relationships, and the dynamics of society.

Another controversial aspect pertains to societal disparities and inequalities. The pursuit of digital immortality requires significant resources, both financial and technological. Access to these resources may be limited to a privileged few, deepening existing social inequalities. The potential emergence of a digital elite, who can afford and access digital immortality, raises concerns about fairness, justice, and the exacerbation of societal divisions.

Balancing the desire for digital immortality with the potential challenges and controversies requires thoughtful consideration and responsible action. Open and inclusive dialogues among scientists, ethicists, policymakers, and y society as a whole are crucial to address these complex issues. Implementing robust ethical frameworks, informed consent processes, and ensuring transparency in the development and use of technologies related to digital immortality can help navigate the challenges and mitigate potential controversies.

The pursuit of digital immortality presents challenges and controversies that span technical, ethical, philosophical, and societal realms. The nature of consciousness, technical limitations, ethical considerations, philosophical debates, and concerns about social disparities all contribute to the complexities surrounding the concept. Engaging in thoughtful and informed

discussions, maintaining ethical guidelines, and ensuring broad societal participation are essential to navigate the pursuit digital immortality in a responsible and inclusive manner.

Chapter 9: The Role of Al in the Quest for Anti-Aging

Al-powered drug discovery and personalized medicine

Artificial intelligence (AI) has emerged as a powerful tool in revolutionizing the field of drug discovery and personalized medicine. By harnessing the vast potential of machine learning, deep learning, and data analytics, Al offers new avenues for accelerating drug development processes, identifying novel therapeutic targets, and tailoring treatments to individual patients.

Time-consuming process, often taking several years and significant financial resources to bring a drug to market. Al technologies streamline this process by analyzing vast amounts of data, including genomic information, protein structures, drug-target interactions, and clinical trial data. Machine learning algorithms can identify patterns, predict drug efficacy and toxicity, and generate novel drug candidates with higher success rates. This expedites the identification and optimization of potential drugs, reducing costs and accelerating the development timeline.

Al enables the identification of novel therapeutic targets by analyzing complex biological data. By integrating multi-omics data, such as genomics, proteomics, and Al-powered drug discovery is transforming the way scientists identify and design potential drugs. Traditional drug discovery is a complex metabolomics, Al algorithms can uncover hidden relationships and identify key molecular pathways involved in disease development and progression. This knowledge allows scientists to identify potential drug targets and develop more targeted therapies, increasing the chances of therapeutic success while minimizing off-target effects.

Personalized medicine, also known as precision medicine, aims to tailor medical treatments to individual patients based on their unique genetic makeup, lifestyle, and disease characteristics. Al plays a pivotal role in advancing personalized medicine by analyzing large-scale patient data, including genomic information, electronic health records, and clinical trial data. Machine learning algorithms can identify patient subgroups, predict disease progression, and recommend personalized treatment plans.

This enables healthcare providers to make informed decisions about the most effective therapies, dosages, and treatment regimens for individual patients, optimizing treatment outcomes and minimizing adverse effects.

Another significant aspect of Al in personalized medicine is predictive analytics. Machine learning models can analyze patient data and generate predictive models for disease onset, progression, and response to treatment. This enables early detection of diseases, facilitates preventive interventions, and improves patient outcomes.

Al algorithms can also analyze real-time patient data, such as wearable device data, to monitor disease progression, track treatment efficacy, and enable timely interventions.

The integration of Al in drug discovery and personalized medicine presents several benefits, including increased efficiency, cost savings, and improved patient outcomes. However, challenges and considerations remain. The quality and diversity of data used to train Al models are crucial for their accuracy and reliability. Ensuring data privacy, security, and ethical considerations is paramount when handling sensitive patient information.

Additionally, the interpretability and explainability of Al models are important for building trust and ensuring transparency in decision-making processes.

Collaboration between Al experts, healthcare professionals, and regulatory bodies is essential to harness the full potential of Al in drug discovery and personalized medicine. Regulatory frameworks must adapt to the rapidly evolving landscape of Al technologies to ensure their safe and responsible deployment.

Continued research, development, and validation of Al models and algorithms are necessary to ensure their robustness and reliability in real-world clinical settings. Al-powered drug discovery and personalized medicine have transformative potential in advancing healthcare. By leveraging the capabilities of Al, scientists

can accelerate drug discovery processes, identify novel therapeutic targets, and design personalized treatment plans.

The integration of Al in drug development and healthcare decision-making has the potential to improve patient outcomes, increase treatment efficacy, and contribute to more targeted and precise medical interventions. As Al technologies continue to evolve, it is crucial to strike a balance between innovation, ethical considerations, and patient safety to realize the full benefits of Al in drug discovery and personalized medicine.

Machine learning algorithms and predictive modeling in anti-aging research

Machine learning algorithms and predictive modeling have emerged as powerful tools in the field of anti-aging research. By analyzing large and complex datasets, these algorithms can uncover patterns, predict outcomes, and provide valuable insights into the aging process.

One of the primary applications of machine learning in anti-aging research is the analysis of genomics data.

Genomic data provides a wealth of information about an individual's genetic makeup, including variations and mutations that may contribute to the aging process. Machine learning algorithms can analyze these vast datasets, identify genetic markers associated with aging-related traits or diseases, and predict an individual's susceptibility to age-related conditions. This information can aid in early detection, intervention, and the development of personalized anti-aging strategies.

Predictive modeling also plays a vital role in understanding the aging process and its impact on health outcomes. By integrating multi-omics data, such as genomics, proteomics, metabolomics, and clinical data, predictive models can identify patterns and relationships between various factors and aging -related outcomes. For example, machine learning algorithms can predict an individual's risk of developing age-related diseases, such as cardiovascular disease, neurodegenerative disorders, or cancer, based on their biological and lifestyle factors. This allows for targeted interventions and preventive

measures to delay or mitigate the onset of age-related conditions.

In the field of longevity research, predictive modeling enables the identification of factors and interventions that contribute to healthy aging and longevity. By analyzing longitudinal data from large cohorts, machine learning algorithms can identify predictors of exceptional longevity and the key lifestyle or genetic factors associated with healthy aging. These insights can guide the development of interventions and personalized anti-aging strategies to promote extended healthspan and improve quality of Life.

By analyzing large databases of chemical compounds, biological targets, and their interactions, algorithms can identify novel drug candidates or repurpose existing drugs for anti-aging purposes. This approach expedites the identification and development of potential interventions, potentially bypassing the traditional trial-and-error process.

While machine learning algorithms and predictive modeling offer immense potential in anti-aging research, challenges and considerations remain. The quality and diversity of data used for training these algorithms are

crucial for their accuracy and generalizability.

Robust datasets that represent diverse populations and account for various confounding factors are essential for reliable predictions and meaningful insights. Ensuring data privacy, security, and ethical considerations in handling sensitive health information are also paramount. Moreover, the interpretability and explainability of machine learning models are important for building trust and facilitating the translation of research findings into clinical practice.

The ability to understand and interpret the factors contributing to predictions allows researchers and healthcare professionals to validate and refine models, as well as ensure the ethical and responsible use of predictive algorithms in healthcare decision-making. Machine learning algorithms and predictive modeling have the potential to revolutionize anti-aging research by enabling the analysis of large and complex datasets, predicting outcomes, and providing valuable insights into the aging process.

By identifying genetic markers, predicting disease risks, and guiding personalized interventions, these technologies contribute to the development of targeted anti-aging strategies and interventions. Continued research, validation, and collaboration among scientists, healthcare professionals, and regulators are essential to harness the full potential of machine learning and predictive modeling in anti-aging research and translate these advancements into improved health outcomes and extended healthspan

The ethical implications of Al-driven decision-making in healthcare

The integration of artificial intelligence (AI) in healthcare has led to significant advancements in diagnosis, treatment, and decision-making.

Al-driven decision-making systems have the potential to improve patient outcomes, enhance efficiency, and optimize resource allocation.

However, the adoption of Al in healthcare also raises complex ethical considerations that must be carefully addressed.

One of the primary ethical concerns is transparency and explainability. Al algorithms often operate as black boxes, making decisions based on complex patterns and correlations within data. The lack of transparency and interpretability in Al decision-making can undermine trust and raise questions about accountability. It is crucial to develop Al systems that are explainable, allowing healthcare professionals and patients to understand how decisions are made and ensuring transparency in the decision-making process.

Another ethical consideration is bias and fairness in Al algorithms. Biases can be inadvertently introduced into Al models if the training data is biased or reflects societal prejudices. This can lead to disparities in the care provided to different populations, exacerbating existing healthcare inequalities. Efforts must be made to identify and address biases in Al algorithms, ensuring fairness and equitable healthcare outcomes for all patients.

Data privacy and security are paramount ethical concerns in Al-driven decision-making. Al algorithms rely on vast amounts of sensitive patient data, including electronic health records, genomic information, and medical imaging. Protecting patient privacy and maintaining the security of healthcare data is essential to prevent unauthorized access, data breaches, or misuse of personal health information. Robust data protection measures and compliance with legal and regulatory frameworks are imperative in Al-driven healthcare systems.

Another ethical dilemma revolves around the delegation of decision-making to Al systems. While Al algorithms can provide valuable insights and recommendations, the ultimate responsibility for healthcare decisions still lies with healthcare professionals. Striking the right balance between human expertise and Al assistance is crucial. Healthcare professionals must maintain their autonomy, critically evaluate Al-generated recommendations, and exercise their judgment to ensure patient well-being.

Informed consent is another ethical consideration in Al-driven decision-making.

Patients have the right to be informed about the involvement of Al systems in their care, including the potential risks, limitations, and alternatives.

Transparent communication regarding the role of Al in decision-making empowers patients to actively participate in their care and make informed choices.

The use of Al algorithms in diagnosis and treatment planning can influence the dynamics of the relationship, potentially altering the balance of power and diminishing the human touch. Healthcare professionals must ensure that the integration of Al does not compromise the quality of the patient-provider relationship, maintaining empathy, communication, and shared decision-making.

Lastly, societal implications of Al-driven decision-making in healthcare must be addressed. The widespread adoption of Al systems may lead to workforce displacement and job changes within the healthcare industry. Ensuring a smooth transition and providing training and support for healthcare professionals affected by Al-driven changes are ethical considerations to be addressed.

While Al-driven decision-making holds immense potential in healthcare, it also brings forth significant ethical implications.

Transparency, fairness, data privacy, informed consent, and the preservation of the patient-provider relationship are key ethical considerations in the design, implementation, and use of AI systems. Striking the right balance between the benefits of AI and the preservation of ethical principles is crucial to harness the potential of AI-driven decision-making in healthcare and ensure that it serves the best interests of patients while upholding ethical standards.

Chapter 10: Embracing Agelessness: A Digital Manifesto

Embracing the digital age as a catalyst for a healthier, longer life

The digital age has revolutionized nearly every aspect of our lives, including healthcare. With the advent of innovative technologies, connectivity, and data-driven insights, we have the opportunity to embrace the digital age as a catalyst for achieving a healthier and longer life. One of the key advantages of the digital age is the availability of vast amounts of health information and resources at our fingertips.

Through the internet and digital platforms individuals have access to a wealth of knowledge about healthy lifestyles, preventive measures, and evidence-based medical research. This empowers people to make informed decisions and take proactive steps towards improving their health. From online health education resources to health-tracking apps, the digital age provides tools to promote self-awareness, education, and engagement in personal well-being.

Digital technologies also enable remote monitoring and telemedicine, transforming the way healthcare is delivered. Telehealth services, virtual consultations, and remote monitoring devices allow individuals to receive timely healthcare interventions without the need for in-person visits. This is especially beneficial for individuals in rural or underserved areas who may have limited access to healthcare facilities.

Remote monitoring devices, such as wearables and connected sensors, enable continuous tracking of vital signs, physical activity, sleep patterns, and other health metrics. This real-time data can facilitate early detection of health issues, preventive interventions, and personalized healthcare management.

The digital age has also given rise to personalized medicine and precision healthcare. By integrating genomic data, electronic health records, and advanced analytics, digital platforms can generate personalized insights and recommendations tailored to an individual's unique characteristics and health needs. Machine learning algorithms can analyze large datasets, identify patterns, and predict disease risks, allowing for targeted interventions and

preventive measures. Personalized medicine holds the promise of optimizing treatment outcomes, minimizing adverse effects, and tailoring interventions to individual patients.

Digital technologies provide avenues for promoting healthy behaviors and fostering community support. Mobile apps, social media platforms, and online communities enable individuals to set health goals, track progress, and connect with like-minded individuals on a journey towards better health. Gamification techniques and virtual challenges make the pursuit of health and wellness engaging and enjoyable. The ability to share experiences, seek support, and access virtual communities can significantly impact motivation and adherence to healthy habits.

Furthermore, the digital age facilitates the integration of artificial intelligence (AI) in healthcare. AI algorithms can analyze large datasets, identify patterns, and provide insights that aid in diagnosis, treatment planning, and decision-making. Machine learning models can predict disease progression, recommend treatment options, and improve patient outcomes. The synergy between AI and human expertise has the potential to enhance medical knowledge, accelerate research, and

improve healthcare delivery.

As we embrace the digital age as a catalyst for a healthier, longer life, it is important to address certain considerations.

Data privacy and security must be ensured to protect sensitive health information and maintain trust in digital healthcare systems. Ethical considerations surrounding AI-driven decision-making and algorithms must be carefully addressed to ensure transparency, fairness, and accountability. Bridging the digital divide to ensure equal access to digital healthcare technologies is also crucial, as disparities in access could exacerbate existing health inequalities.

The digital age offers unprecedented opportunities to achieve a healthier and longer life. Through access to health information, telemedicine, personalized medicine, and the integration of AI, we can harness the power of digital technologies to promote well-being, prevent diseases, and optimize healthcare outcomes. Embracing the digital age as a catalyst for a healthier, longer life requires responsible deployment of technologies, addressing ethical and privacy considerations, and ensuring equitable access to digital healthcare resources.

By embracing the digital age and leveraging its potential, we can empower individuals, transform healthcare systems, and pave the way for an extended healthspan and improved quality of life.

The importance of education, lifestyle choices, and mental resilience in anti-aging

When it comes to the pursuit of healthy aging and promoting well-being throughout life, education, lifestyle choices, and mental resilience play crucial roles. These factors have a profound impact on our physical, cognitive, and emotional well-being, contributing to our ability to age gracefully and maintain a high quality of life.

Education is a powerful tool in promoting healthy aging. It equips individuals with knowledge, skills, and awareness necessary to make informed decisions about their health. Education empowers individuals to understand the importance of preventive measures, engage in healthy behaviors, and navigate the complexities of the healthcare system. Through education, individuals can acquire knowledge about healthy eating, regular exercise, disease prevention, and the benefits of a well-balanced lifestyle. Moreover, education fosters a lifelong learning mindset, enabling individuals to stay updated with advancements in healthcare, technology, and self-care practices.

Lifestyle choices are instrumental in determining the trajectory of aging and overall well-being. Engaging in regular physical activity, maintaining a balanced diet, and avoiding harmful habits such as smoking or excessive alcohol consumption are essential components of a healthy lifestyle.

Physical activity helps maintain muscle strength, cardiovascular health, and bone density, while a nutritious diet provides essential nutrients and antioxidants that support cellular health and combat age-related oxidative stress. Making conscious choices to prioritize sleep, manage stress, and engage in social connections also contribute to overall well-being and healthy aging. Mental resilience, encompassing psychological well-being and cognitive fitness, is a vital aspect of anti-aging.

Cultivating mental resilience involves developing emotional intelligence, adaptability, and coping mechanisms to navigate life's challenges. It entails maintaining a positive mindset, managing stress effectively, and fostering social connections and support networks.

Mental resilience contributes to reduced risk of cognitive decline, improved emotional well-being, and enhanced overall quality of life. Activities such as mindfulness practices, cognitive training, and engaging in hobbies that promote mental stimulation are beneficial for maintaining cognitive function and emotional balance. Furthermore, education, lifestyle choices, and mental resilience are interdependent and mutually reinforcing.

Education provides individuals with the knowledge and awareness to make informed lifestyle choices that support healthy aging. On the other hand, adopting a healthy lifestyle and nurturing mental resilience positively impacts cognitive function and can enhance the capacity for lifelong learning. Together, these factors create a positive feedback loop, promoting holistic well-being and anti-aging effects.

Continual learning, staying informed about emerging research, and adjusting lifestyle choices to align with evolving knowledge are crucial for maintaining optimal health and well-being throughout the aging process. Education, lifestyle choices, and mental resilience are essential pillars of anti-aging efforts. Education empowers individuals with knowledge, enabling informed decision-making and lifelong learning.

Making conscious lifestyle choices that prioritize physical health, nutrition, and emotional well-being contributes to healthy aging. Building mental resilience fosters cognitive fitness and emotional balance, enhancing overall quality of life. Embracing education, lifestyle choices, and mental resilience as integral components of anti-aging strategies empowers individuals to proactively promote their well-being, age gracefully, and enjoy an extended healthspan.

Navigating the brave new world of anti-aging in the digital era

In our increasingly digital world, the pursuit of anti-aging has taken on a new dimension. Technology and the digital landscape have opened up exciting possibilities for promoting healthy aging, extending healthspan, and enhancing well-being. However, navigating this brave new world of anti-aging in the digital realm requires careful consideration and awareness of the opportunities and challenges it presents.

One of the key aspects of navigating the digital world of anti-aging is staying informed. The rapid advancement of technology means that new interventions, products, and digital platforms aimed at promoting healthy aging constantly emerge. Keeping up-to-date with the latest research, evidence-based practices, and reputable sources of information is crucial to make informed decisions about anti-aging strategies.

Engaging with reliable online resources, subscribing to newsletters from trusted organizations, and following reputable experts in the field can help individuals stay abreast of the latest developments. Another important consideration is to critically evaluate the digital tools and interventions available for anti-aging. The digital landscape offers a myriad of health apps, wearable devices, and online platforms that claim to enhance well- being and slow down the aging process.

However, not all interventions are created equal, and it is essential to assess their credibility, scientific basis, and user reviews before embracing them. Reading user testimonials, seeking recommendations from healthcare professionals, and considering evidence-based research can help individuals make informed choices about digital interventions. Data privacy and security are paramount when navigating the digital world of anti-aging.

Many digital tools and platforms collect and store personal health information, such as activity levels, sleep patterns, and vital signs. It is crucial to understand the privacy policies, data sharing practices, and security measures employed by these platforms to protect sensitive health information.

Taking precautions such as using strong passwords, enabling two-factor authentication, and being mindful of sharing personal information online can help safeguard privacy in the digital realm. Building a support network and engaging with online communities can provide valuable resources and encouragement along the anti-aging journey.

Connecting with like-minded individuals who share similar goals and challenges can foster a sense of community and provide a platform for sharing experiences, seeking advice, and finding motivation. Online forums, social media groups, and virtual communities centered around healthy aging can serve as valuable sources of support and knowledge. In addition, it is essential to strike a balance between digital engagement and real-world experiences.

While the digital world offers numerous tools and platforms for anti-aging, it is crucial not to overlook the importance of offline interactions, physical activity, and real-world connections. Maintaining a balanced lifestyle that includes face-to-face interactions, outdoor activities, and other non-digital experiences is vital for overall well-being and mental health.

Lastly, practicing digital wellness is important in navigating the digital world of anti-aging. Setting boundaries for screen time, practicing mindfulness, and taking breaks from digital devices contribute to a healthy relationship with technology. Being mindful of the impact of digital media on mental well-being, managing information overload, and fostering a healthy balance between online and offline activities are essential for maintaining a positive and productive digital experience.

Navigating the brave new world of anti-aging in the digital realm requires staying informed, critically evaluating digital interventions, prioritizing data privacy, building support networks, and maintaining a balanced digital lifestyle. By harnessing the power of the digital world while being mindful of its potential pitfalls, individuals can effectively navigate the digital landscape and embrace its potential for promoting healthy aging, extending healthspan, and enhancing overall well-being.

Epilogue: Beyond the Horizon

Speculating on the future of anti-aging and its impact on society

Speculating on the future of anti-aging and its impact on society unveils a world of

transformative possibilities. As advancements in biotechnology, regenerative medicine, and digital technologies continue to accelerate, the boundaries of human lifespan and health are being redefined.

The potential to delay, reverse, or even prevent age-related diseases and deterioration holds promise for extending healthy lifespans and improving the quality of life for individuals worldwide. A society with extended lifespans could witness profound shifts in social structures, relationships, and cultural norms. It may require reimagining traditional milestones like retirement, career trajectories, and intergenerational dynamics.

Furthermore, the concept of age itself could be reshaped, challenging existing notions of identity and societal expectations. However, as we explore the future of anti-aging, it is crucial to address ethical considerations, including equitable access to these advancements, the distribution of resources, and the potential for exacerbating social inequalities. By engaging in thoughtful discussions and collective decision-making, we can shape a future where anti-aging interventions foster well-being, social cohesion, and a more inclusive and fulfilling society.

Embracing the possibilities of a digitally empowered and ageless future

Embracing the possibilities of a digitally empowered and ageless future opens doors to a world of endless potential and boundless opportunities. In this future, digital technologies seamlessly integrate with our lives, enhancing our well-being, connecting us globally, and empowering us to thrive at any age.

Digital platforms offer personalized healthcare solutions, allowing us to monitor our health, access virtual care, and make informed decisions about our well-being. Connectivity fosters intergenerational connections, enabling the exchange of knowledge, experiences, and perspectives. Lifelong learning becomes the norm, as individuals engage in continuous education, skill development, and personal growth.

Age is no longer a barrier to pursuing passions, contributing to society, or embarking on new adventures. The digitally empowered and ageless future embraces diversity, inclusivity, and equitable access to resources and opportunities. It encourages intergenerational collaboration, innovation, and the celebration of the richness that comes with a diverse and vibrant society. By embracing this future, we can forge a path where individuals can lead fulfilling, purposeful lives, making significant contributions to their communities and embracing the endless possibilities that the digital age offers.

About the Author

Mazen Kaldas is a certified fitness professional and a nutrition enthusiast, he spent years studying the intricate relationship between nutrition, exercise, and the aging process. Drawing from extensive research and personal experience, Mazen offers practical insights and evidence-based strategies to optimize health and slow down the effects of aging. He has successfully guided countless individuals on their journey to unlock their full potential to lead their lives towards a much improved well-being. Whether it's developing personalized meal plans, designing effective workout routines, or providing expert advice on supplementation, he strives to educate and inspire others to make lasting positive changes to enhance their vitality and age gracefully.